JOSEPH MIDTHUN   SAMUEL HITI

BUILDING BLOCKS OF SCIENCE

and how it changes

WORLD BOOK

a Scott Fetzer company
Chicago
www.worldbook.com

World Book, Inc.
233 N. Michigan Avenue
Chicago, IL 60601
U.S.A.

For information about other World Book publications, visit our website at http://www.worldbook.com or call 1-800-WORLDBK (967-5325).

For information about sales to schools and libraries, call 1-800-975-3250 (United States); 1-800-837-5365 (Canada).

Library of Congress Cataloging-in-Publication Data

Matter and how it changes.
        p. cm. -- (Building blocks of science)
    Includes index.
    Summary: "A graphic nonfiction volume that introduces physical and chemical changes of matter. Features include several photographic pages, a glossary, additional resource list, and an index"-- Provided by publisher.
    ISBN 978-0-7166-1428-9
    1. Matter--Constitution--Juvenile literature.
I. World Book, Inc.
QC173.16.M378 2012
530.41--dc23
                                        2011025904
Building Blocks of Science
Set ISBN: 978-0-7166-1420-3 (print, hc.)

Also available as:
ISBN: 978-0-7166-1470-8 (pbk.)

E-book editions:
ISBN 978-0-7166-1867-6 (EPUB3)
ISBN 978-0-7166-1446-3 (PDF)

Acknowledgments:

Created by Samuel Hiti and Joseph Midthun.
Art by Samuel Hiti. Written by Joseph Midthun.

© Hugh Threlfall, Alamy Images 9; © Photofusion Picture Library/Alamy Images 8; © Stephen Harrison, Alamy Images 8; © Dreamstime 14, 24, 25; © Shutterstock 15, 25; WORLD BOOK Illustration 8, 9

Printed in China by Leo Paper Products, LTD., Heshan Guangdong
3rd printing June 2014

ATTENTION, READER!

Some characters in this series throw large objects from tall buildings, play with fire, ride on bicycle handlebars, and perform other dangerous acts. However, they are CARTOON CHARACTERS. Please do not try any of these things at home because you could seriously harm yourself—or others around you!

STAFF
Executive Committee
President: Donald D. Keller
Vice President and Editor in Chief: Paul A. Kobasa
Vice President, Sales & Marketing: Sean Lockwood
Vice President, International: Richard Flower
Director, Human Resources: Bev Ecker

Editorial
Manager, Supplementary Publications: Cassie Mayer
Writer and Letterer: Joseph Midthun
Editors: Mike DuRoss and Brian Johnson
Researcher: Annie Brodsky
Manager, Contracts & Compliance (Rights & Permissions): Loranne K. Shields

Manufacturing/Pre-Press/Graphics and Design
Director: Carma Fazio
Manufacturing Manager: Steven Hueppchen
Production/Technology Manager: Anne Fritzinger
Proofreader: Emilie Schrage
Senior Manager, Graphics and Design: Tom Evans
Coordinator, Design Development and Production: Brenda B. Tropinski
Book Design: Samuel Hiti
Photographs Editor: Kathy Creech

TABLE OF CONTENTS

There is a glossary on page 30. Terms defined in the glossary are in type **that looks like this** on their first appearance.

CHANGING MATTER

Have you ever wondered how water turns into ice?

When you fill up a tray with water and put it into the freezer...

Hop

Tump

...the water changes from a liquid into a solid.

There are three basic **states of matter:** solids, liquids, and gases.

The molecules in a SOLID vibrate. They are arranged in a repeating pattern, like soldiers marching together.

The molecules in a LIQUID move more freely, like people walking in a large group.

The molecules in a GAS are faster. They move even more freely, like people skating in a park.

So what causes matter to change states?

The state of all matter depends on its temperature.

Temperature is a measure of how much heat something contains.

11

...AND BACK AND FORTH

Matter can change back and forth between states. This happens around the world every day.

As the sun heats a body of water, the liquid water changes into water vapor.

As water vapor rises into the sky, it begins to cool down. As it cools, the water vapor molecules slow down and pack together into tiny droplets of liquid water.

These tiny droplets make clouds.

The tiny droplets stick together and form larger droplets. These droplets fall back to Earth as rain.

If it is cold enough outside, rain can freeze as it falls, changing from a liquid into a solid—snow!

SCOOP

CHEMICAL CHANGES

So far we've talked about physical changes to matter.

When I carved the sculpture, I didn't change the basic properties of wood.

But what happens when I toss wood into a fire?

whoop

Fire causes the wood to burn. This is a **chemical change**.

A chemical change causes different kinds of matter to form.

Smoke and ash are made from the carbon, hydrogen, and oxygen atoms that were in the tree.

Chemical changes are more common than you might think. Here are some other examples of chemical changes:

When humans eat food, their bodies break down the food into basic **nutrients** that are used for energy.

Green plants use the energy from the sun to combine carbon dioxide and water to make "food" and store it.

Plants use the food energy to live and grow.

PHOTOSYNTHESIS

Humans and other animals can then **absorb** that energy by eating plants or by eating animals that eat plants. They can also release the energy by burning the plant.

COOKING

Food spoils when the tiny living things called **microbes** multiply on the food and begin to eat it.

Microbes produce gases and other chemicals, causing changes in flavor or odor. Rotten food smells bad because of the gases given off by microbes.

YEECCH!

FOOD SPOILAGE

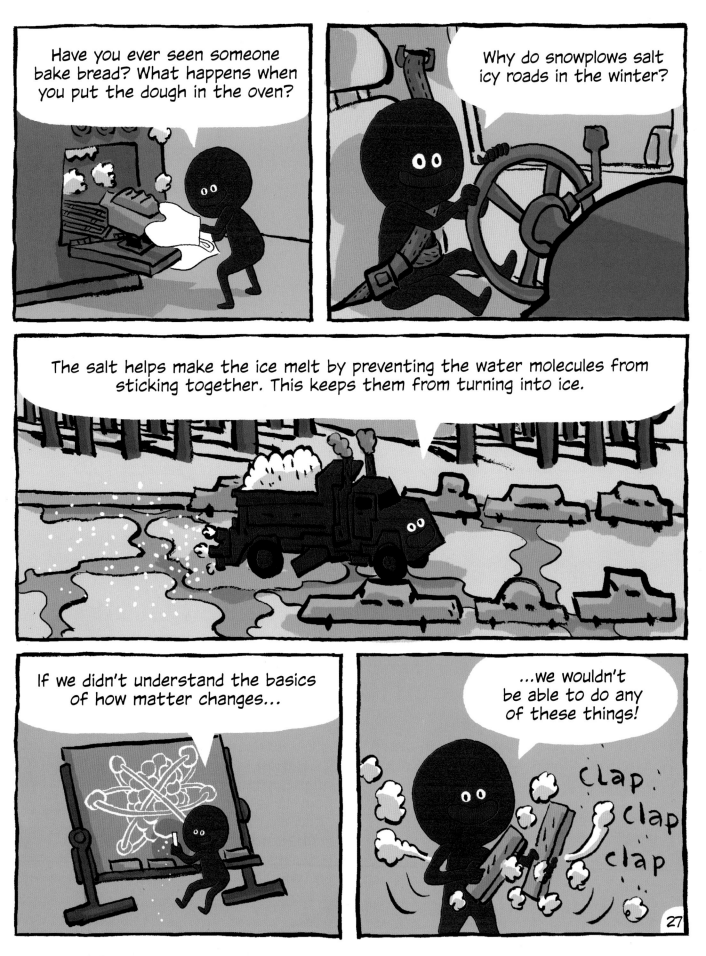

SUPER STATES

Scientists study matter and its different states in laboratories around the world.

They have even discovered some other states of matter!

Super-cold substances create an unusual state of matter.

Superfluids are created by cooling atoms to extremely low temperatures.

A superfluid is a liquid that can behave like a gas.

Liquid Gas

Helium in a superfluid state can creep up the side of its container and crawl over the lip!

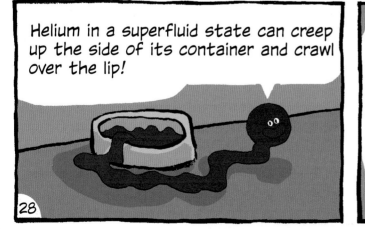

Helium is lighter than air. It is the only **element** that never turns into a solid.

POP

GLOSSARY

absorb to take in and hold rather than reflect.

atom one of the basic units of matter.

chemical change a change in which one substance is converted into one or more substances with different properties.

condensation the changing of a gas or a vapor into a liquid.

element a substance made of only one kind of atom.

evaporate to change from a liquid into a gas.

matter what all things are made of.

microbe a living organism of very small size.

molecule two or more atoms chemically bonded together.

nutrient a nourishing substance, especially as an element or ingredient of food.

physical change a change in which matter changes shape or form.

property a quality or characteristic of something.

solution a mixture in which one substance is dissolved (mixed completely) in another.

states of matter the different forms of matter. The most familiar are solid, liquid, and gas.

suspension a heterogeneous (uneven) mixture of a liquid and a solid in which the solid settles to the bottom if left undisturbed.

water vapor water in the state of a gas.

FIND OUT MORE

Books

Changing States: Solids, Liquids, and Gases by Will Hurd (Heinemann Library, 2009)

Look How It Changes by June Young (Children's Press, 2006)

Matter: See It, Touch It, Taste It, Smell It by Darlene R. Stille and Sheree Boyd (Picture Window Books, 2004)

Melting, Freezing, and Boiling: Science Projects with Matter by Robert Gardner (Enslow Elementary, 2006)

Mixing and Separating by Chris Oxlade (Crabtree Publishing, 2008)

What Is a Gas? by Jennifer Boothroyd (Lerner Publications Co., 2007)

What's the Matter in Mr. Whisker's Room? by Michael Elsohn Ross and Paul Meisel (Candlewick Press, 2004)

Websites

Chem4Kids: States of Matter
http://www.chem4kids.com/files/matter_states.html
Learn more about the states of matter, and how matter moves from one state to another, at this fun and educational chemistry site.

The Exploratorium: Science Snacks About Fluids
http://www.exploratorium.edu/snacks/iconfluids.html
Explore water in its liquid and gas states through these simple, illustrated experiments.

KidZone: The Water Cycle
http://www.kidzone.ws/water/
Work through the stages of the water cycle at this educational website.

Molecularium
http://www.molecularium.com/kidsite.html
At this website, you can travel through the three states of matter with an atomic cast of characters, and build your own molecules in the nanolab.

Science Kids: Chemistry
http://www.sciencekids.co.nz/gamesactivities.html
Play games with solids, liquids, and gases at this educational website that brings science learners together from all over the world.

Strange Matter
http://www.StrangeMatterExhibit.com/
What makes up all the things around us? What makes different materials so different? Find out more about matter and materials at this website.

Study Jams: Solids, Liquids, and Gases
http://teacher.scholastic.com/activities/studyjams/matter_states/
At this site, you can follow along with videos, karaoke, quizzes, and vocabulary exercises to learn about the three states of matter.

TryScience
http://www.tryscience.org/home.html
This site offers both online and offline instructions for such fun states-of-matter experiments as "Water Cycle in a Bag" and "Got Gas?"

INDEX